THE
INSIDE-OUTSIDE
BOOK OF
WASHINGTON, D.C.

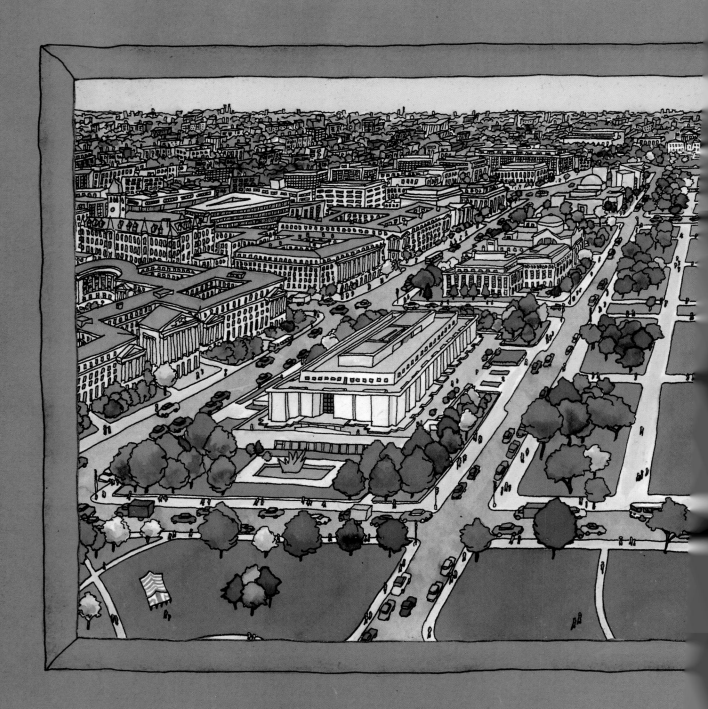

THE INSIDE-OUTSID

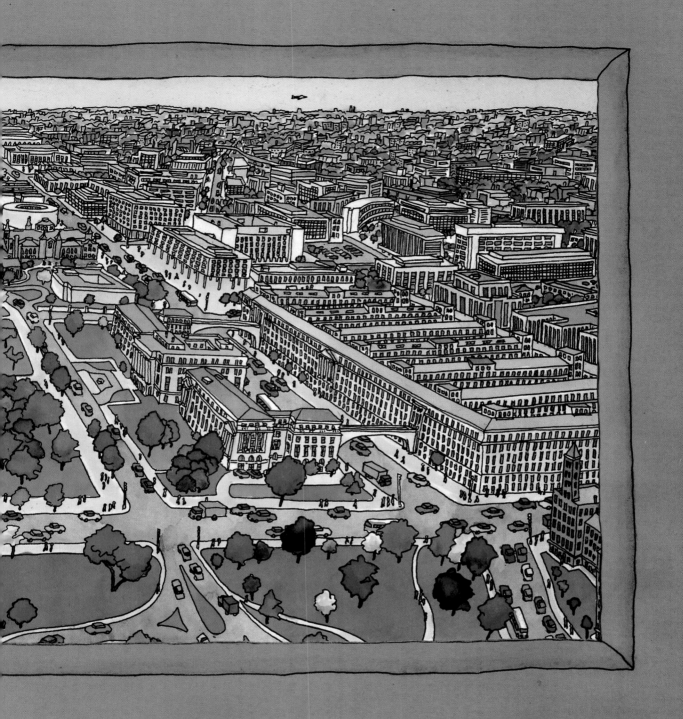

OOK OF
VASHINGTON, D.C.

ROXIE MUNRO

A PUFFIN UNICORN

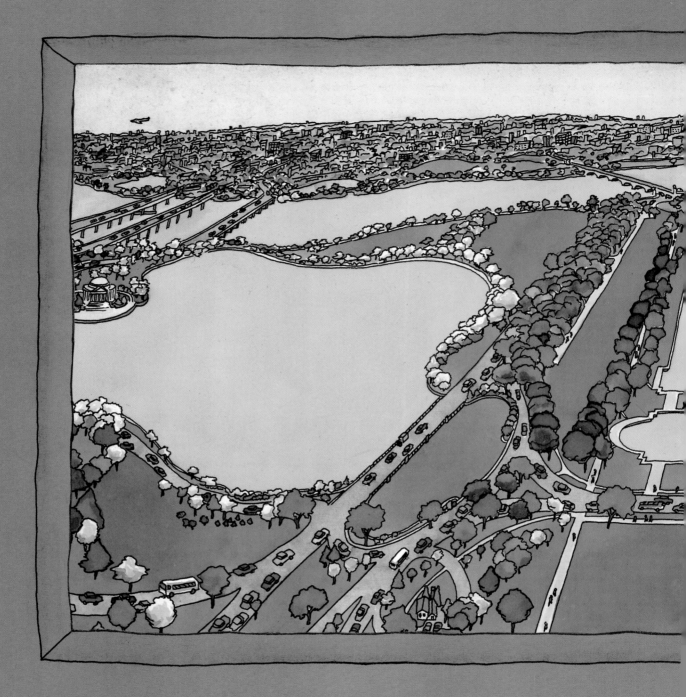

PUFFIN UNICORN BOOKS

Published by the Penguin Group
Penguin Books USA Inc., 375 Hudson Street, New York, New York 10014, U.S.A.
Penguin Books Ltd, 27 Wrights Lane, London W8 5TZ, England
Penguin Books Australia Ltd, Ringwood, Victoria, Australia
Penguin Books Canada Ltd, 10 Alcorn Avenue, Toronto, Ontario, Canada M4V 3B2
Penguin Books (N.Z.) Ltd, 182-190 Wairau Road, Auckland 10, New Zealand
Penguin Books Ltd, Registered Offices: Harmondsworth, Middlesex, England

Library of Congress number 86-24267   ISBN 0-14-054940-4

Published in the United States by Dutton Children's Books,
a division of Penguin Books USA Inc.
Designer: Isabel Warren-Lynch
Printed in Hong Kong by South China Printing Co.
First Puffin Unicorn Edition 1993   10 9 8 7 6 5 4 3 2 1

THE INSIDE-OUTSIDE BOOK OF WASHINGTON, D.C. is also
available in hardcover from Dutton Children's Books.

To my mother and father

Thanks to Donna Brooks, my editor, and Bo Zaunders;
Suzanne Wilson of the Bureau of Engraving and Printing;
Andrea Mitchell of NBC News; and to Ann Munro Wood
and the folks at WUSA–TV 9.

The Library of Congress

The Supreme Court of the United States

The Bureau of Engraving and Printing

The Organization of American States

The National Air and Space Museum

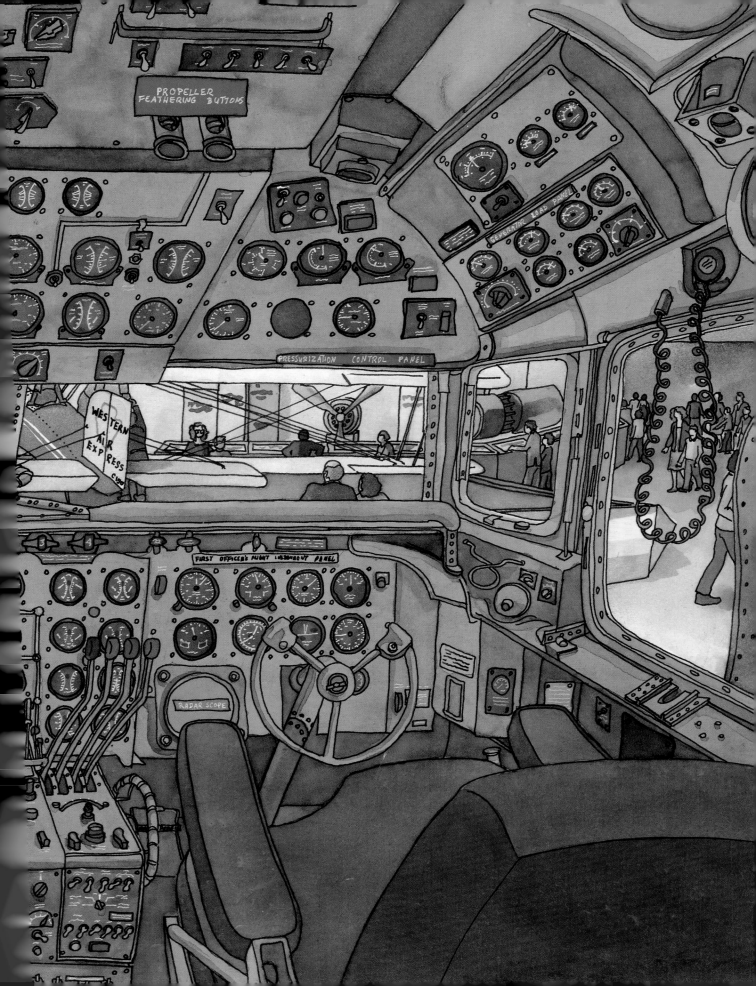

The White House, East Room

The Washington Post

Robert F. Kennedy Memorial Stadium

The United States Capitol, Senate Wing

The Lincoln Memorial

WASHINGTON MONUMENT (opening pages). Built between 1848 and 1885, this luminous structure commemorates the first president of the United States. Delay, lack of funds, and the pragmatism of the Army Corps of Engineers streamlined the original elaborate design. The result is a classically proportioned obelisk of Maryland marble that rises to nearly 556 feet. The 897 steps to the top challenged generations of schoolchildren, but visitors now must take the elevator. Views are spectacular looking east (art) to the Capitol and west (art) to the Lincoln Memorial. Open every day except Christmas.

LIBRARY OF CONGRESS. Founded as the reference library for Congress in 1800, the library also serves the nation as a whole. The original building (art), completed in 1897 on Capitol grounds, is one of the grandest architectural monuments of 19th-century America. At the heart of the library is the Rotunda Reading Room (art), decorated in a flow of ornamentation by American artists. The library collection numbers 80 million items stretching along 532 miles of shelves. Open every day except Christmas and New Year's Day.

SUPREME COURT. Established by Article III of the Constitution, the Court gained stature equal to that of the executive and legislative branches through the bold judicial review of John Marshall. "A more imposing judicial power was never constituted by any people," noted the 19th-century observer Alexis de Tocqueville. The first Court assembled in New York City in 1790. Now it convenes in the Court's permanent home, a neoclassical building (art) east of the Capitol, designed by Cass Gilbert and completed in 1935. More than 5,000 civil and criminal cases are filed each year; about 150 to 175 are granted review, argued, and decided. The media use courtroom artists to depict legal proceedings, because cameras are not allowed. Visitors may be admitted to the chambers (art) on Monday through Wednesday during the 2-week period of each month that the court sits.

BUREAU OF ENGRAVING AND PRINTING. This is where our money is made. Housed in two buildings with a floor space of 25 acres, the bureau employs 3,000 people and operates around the clock mainly to print U.S. paper money in denominations of $1, $5, $10, $20, $50, and $100. After printing, the money is cut and checked for flaws (art), then overprinted with seals and serial numbers, and cut again. The bureau also designs, engraves, and prints about 800 other items, including White House invitations and 31 billion postage stamps yearly. Tours offered at 14th and C Streets SW.

ORGANIZATION OF AMERICAN STATES. Dedicated to promoting peace, security, and development among the people of the Americas, the OAS is made up of over 30 member nations from North, South, and Central America and the Caribbean. Located at Constitution Avenue and 17th Street, the building (art) blends influences from the native Indian cultures of the Americas with a neoclassical style. The art shows a parade of member-nation costumes in the grand Hall of the Americas during a model OAS General Assembly, a simulation of official proceedings for students. Open weekdays.

AIR AND SPACE MUSEUM. Ten million visitors a year flock to this most popular museum in the world, part of the Smithsonian, to view aircraft, spacecraft, and rockets representing 80 years of aerospace technology. Some are familiar as great symbols of our age—the Wright brothers' plane, the *Spirit of St. Louis, Apollo 11*. In the Hall of Air Transportation (art) hangs a Douglas DC-3, the first plane to make air transportation profitable and the heaviest airplane suspended in the museum. Visitors may enter the cockpit of the American Airlines DC-7 flagship *Vermont* (art). Open daily except Christmas.

WHITE HOUSE, EAST ROOM. The home of every president except Washington (who chose the site) is also the oldest public building in the capital and probably the most familiar house in America. John and Abigail Adams dried their laundry in the unfinished East Room. Now that room (to which Ulysses S. Grant added the chandeliers) is used for large gatherings, including press conferences (art), after which correspondents give stand-up reports in front of the North Portico (art). In the control room of a local TV station (art), the edited network coverage is received and relayed to homes throughout the community. Tours available.

THE WASHINGTON POST. The first edition of the *Post,* founded in 1877, had 4 pages and cost 3¢. Joseph Pulitzer wrote for the *Post,* Teddy Roosevelt contributed stories, and in its honor John Philip Sousa composed "The Washington Post" march. The art shows presses, 2 stories high and ½ block long, in the basement of the building between L and M Streets at 15th. The fastest presses can print, cut, and fold 65,000 newspapers an hour. Over 8,000 carriers ensure early morning delivery to homes throughout the area (art). Tours available.

RFK STADIUM. Two miles due east of the Capitol, this 55,000-seat, cantilevered stadium is the home of the 1983 Super Bowl Champions, the Washington Redskins. Scheduled home games of the popular Redskins (frequently attended by presidents) have been sold out for over 20 years. The art shows the famous Redskins–Cowboys rivalry.

CAPITOL. The building that houses the Senate and the House of Representatives (and from 1860-1935, the Supreme Court) is the work of 9 architects. Its cast-iron dome, the model for many state capitols, took shape during the Civil War. "If the people see the Capitol going on," said President Lincoln, "it is a sign the Union shall go on." Visitors may take tours and obtain passes to the Senate (art) or House galleries to watch the legislative branch of the government in action.

LINCOLN MEMORIAL. The colossal figure seated within Henry Bacon's neoclassical Greek temple took Daniel Chester French 13 years to sculpt and stonecutters 4 years to carve. Commanding a view of the reflecting pool, the Washington Monument, and the Capitol beyond, the memorial occupies a site with "undisputed domination over a large area, together with a certain dignified isolation," as the founding commission stipulated. Its walls are surrounded by 32 columns, representing the 32 states in the Union at the time of Lincoln's death. Inside, flanked by the Gettysburg Address and the Second Inaugural, French's figure of Lincoln evokes the greatness and humility of this supreme statesman, whom Walt Whitman described as having a face like a "Hoosier Michael Angelo." Its beauty and purity of design make the memorial one of the most moving national shrines to emerge in the modern age.

WHITE HOUSE, SOUTH LAWN (covers). In recent years, the presidential helicopter has landed and taken off from the South Lawn (art). The wrought-iron fence (art) was put in by FDR; Harry Truman added the second-story balcony of the South Portico.

DUE DATE

NO 18 '97			
MR 17 '08			
	201-6503		Printed in USA